IF YOU WERE A KID IN THE
Wild West

BY TRACEY BAPTISTE • ILLUSTRATED BY JASON RAISH

CHILDREN'S PRESS® An Imprint of Scholastic Inc.

Content Consultant
James Marten, PhD, Professor and Chair, History Department, Marquette University, Milwaukee, Wisconsin

NOTE TO THE READER, PARENT, LIBRARIAN, AND TEACHER: This book combines a historical fiction narrative with nonfiction fact boxes. While all the nonfiction fact boxes are historically accurate and true, the fiction comes solely from the imaginations of the author and illustrator.

Photos ©: 9: Carol M. Highsmith/Library of Congress; 11: Erwin E. Smith/Library of Congress; 13: Strobridge & Co./Library of Congress; 15: John C. H. Grabill/Library of Congress; 17: John van Hasselt - Corbis/Getty Images; 19: Alfred A. Hart/Library of Congress; 21: Americanspirit/Dreamstime; 23: Lewis Wickes Hine/Library of Congress; 25: Three Lions/Getty Images; 27: GlobalP/iStockphoto.

Library of Congress Cataloging-in-Publication Data
Names: Baptiste, Tracey, author. | Raish, Jason, illustrator.
Title: If you were a kid in the wild west / by Tracey Baptiste ; illustrated by Jason Raish.
Description: New York, NY : Children's Press, an imprint of Scholastic Inc., 2018. |
Series: If you were a kid | Includes bibliographical references and index.
Identifiers: LCCN 2017032487 | ISBN 9780531232156 (library binding) | ISBN 9780531243138 (pbk.)
Subjects: LCSH: West (U.S.)—History—Juvenile literature. | Frontier and pioneer life—West (U.S.)—
Juvenile literature. | Children—West (U.S.)—History—19th century—Juvenile literature.
Classification: LCC F591 .B24 2018 | DDC 978—dc23
LC record available at https://lccn.loc.gov/2017032487

Scholastic Inc., 557 Broadway, New York, NY 10012

1 2 3 4 5 6 7 8 9 10 R 27 26 25 24 23 22 21 20 19 18

TABLE OF CONTENTS

4

A Different Way of Life

Many people moved to the American West between 1865 and 1900. This was right after the end of the U.S. Civil War (1861–1865). White **settlers** were seeking their fortune as farmers, ranchers, or gold miners. Former enslaved people left the **racism** of the Southern states for all-black towns. Chinese people came to work, mostly on the transcontinental railroad, which connected the coasts. Japanese people **migrated** to California to work on farms. They all met Mexican and Native American people who already lived there. This period of westward **expansion** is known as the Wild West era. It is called "wild" because there were few towns or cities. The animals there were untamed. Laws were rarely followed.

Turn the page to set off on your own Wild West adventure! You will see that life today is a lot different than it was in the past.

Meet Kate!

Kate Smith's family owns a general store in Dodge City, Kansas. Kate is the oldest of six children. Each of them helps out at the store. It's very busy there now because it is cattle drive season. That means groups of cowboys are passing through town all the time. The cowboys lead huge numbers of longhorn steers to be shipped on the railroad. There is a lot to do, but Kate wishes she could go to school instead . . .

Meet Nat!

After slavery was **abolished**, Nat Jackson's family thought about leaving the South. But Nat's father found work as a cowboy on a Texas ranch. He earned just as much money as the white cowboys. This is Nat's first cattle drive. He's joining his father and the rest of the cowboys on the trip to Dodge City. His job is to be a wrangler, which means he has to chase after stray animals. It's hard and dusty work, but good practice for being a cowboy one day . . .

Kate scrambled up a ladder to get a jar of her mother's peaches for a customer.

"Get two more from the storeroom, Jane," she called down to her sister.

With so many people in town for the cattle drive, items were going fast. Kate was trying to be quick and helpful. But it was hard to keep up with everything.

"Watch out!" Kate cried as the jar slipped out of her fingers. Jane caught it. Whew!

ONE-STOP SHOPPING

It was difficult to find many everyday items in the Wild West. People traveling the trails loaded up their wagons, but they could not carry much. Also, things were broken or lost on the trip. General stores carried everything from food to tools to fabric. In mining towns, stores also carried pickaxes and shovels. Store owners could get rich setting very high prices for their goods.

If something wasn't in stock at the general store, people in town had to place special orders to get what they wanted.

Nat and the cowboys were just about in Dodge City when a cloud of dust rose up ahead.

"Stampede!" the trail boss called out.

Nat saw a line of wagons driving through the herd of steers. He realized that the animals must have been spooked by the wagon train. The cowboys sprang into action, but one steer got away.

"Do your job, wrangler," Nat's father shouted. Nat went after the loose steer at top speed.

LIFE ON A CATTLE TRAIL

There were several jobs on a cattle drive. The trail boss led the team and chose the path. The cook drove a wagon filled with food. He also hunted animals to get meat. Lead riders rode in front of the cattle herd. Outriders rode along the sides. Drag riders brought up the rear. There was also a wrangler. This was a young boy who went after strays.

A cowboy takes a break near his horse.

Kate's youngest brother, Billy, moaned and coughed as he leaned against a stack of flour bags. His skin was burning hot. Oh no, Kate thought. He's sick!

A salesman was outside shouting about **miracle** cures. Kate ran out to buy something for her brother's cough. As she got close, a young cowboy rode in front of her at top speed. She fell backward onto the ground. Surprised, the salesman dropped his bottles. They spilled onto the dusty road.

NOT SO MIRACULOUS

Salesmen traveled from town to town offering cures for everything from headaches to serious illnesses. These **patent medicines** were usually not real. The salesmen often paid someone to pretend to be cured after taking the medicine. This convinced people to buy the medicine. In the 1900s, newspapers began reporting this practice. Soon, everyone knew better than to buy things from traveling medicine sellers.

Advertisements made patent medicines seem better than they really were.

DR BRUESS' POWERFUL PENETRATING PEERLESS REMEDY

THE BEST LINIMENT ON EARTH

DR BRUESS PPP REMEDY

CURES ALL PAIN

"I'm very sorry!" Nat said as he got down from his horse.

"I needed those to help my brother," Kate said angrily. "He's sick."

"Those are fake," Nat explained. "You should get a doctor." At Nat's words, the medicine man quickly ran off.

Nat helped Kate up. "What's the hurry anyway?" she asked.

"One of our steers ran away," said Nat.

"Check down by the river," Kate said. "Tired animals usually end up there."

COWBOYS

The word *cowboy* comes from the Spanish word *vaquero*. The first cowboys were Mexican. Later, other cowboys wore the same ponchos and wide-brimmed hats that the Mexicans used. This clothing protected them from sun, wind, rain, and snow as they worked. It was not unusual to see cowboys of different races working together. From 1865 to the late 1880s, about one in three cowboys was Mexican or African American.

Cowboys were highly skilled horse riders.

Kate ran back inside. Her mother was putting a damp cloth on Billy's head. "I tried to get medicine," Kate explained. "But someone rode through looking for a missing steer."

"It could be cattle **rustlers**," said Kate's mother. "This town has so many people now. It's hard to know who you can trust." She told Kate to lock the windows and the storeroom door.

THE LAW OF THE WEST

Dodge City, Kansas, was one of the most popular "cow towns" of the Wild West. It also had a reputation for unlawfulness. Most people in Dodge City were more interested in making money than obeying the law. Some of the most famous lawmen and gunfighters spent time there. They included Doc Holliday and Wyatt Earp.

John Henry "Doc" Holliday was a famous gambler and gunfighter. He got his nickname from being a dentist.

As Nat rode toward the river, he passed two Chinese men carrying tools.

"Excuse me," Nat said. "Have you seen a longhorn running loose?"

The men pointed down the hill.

"Thanks!" Nat called out as he rode. Soon, he came across a small pond. Nearby, in a muddy patch, was the missing cow.

MAKING THE RAILS

Railroads made it easier for people to travel to the West. They also led to faster communication and an easier way to ship goods westward. The transcontinental railroad was started in 1863 and finished in 1869. It connected the East to the West with a 1,912-mile (3,077-kilometer) route. Two-thirds of the workers on the project were Chinese. Other railroads were built later to connect more cities. One of those was the Santa Fe Railroad through Dodge City.

Workers construct a section of the transcontinental railroad in Nevada.

From the locked store, Kate watched other children on their way to school.

"I wish we could go," she said to her younger siblings.

"I like working in the store," Jane said. She stacked some fresh jars of peaches.

"You can go when we're not so busy," their mother said.

Just then a customer knocked on the door. Kate let him in. Maybe she would have time to go to school tomorrow.

WILD WEST EDUCATION

Many Wild West towns didn't have a schoolhouse. Children often had other work to do. In towns that did have schools, the teacher might be as young as 15. Students of all ages learned basic skills such as reading, writing, and math. They were taught in one-room schoolhouses.

This is how the first one-room schoolhouse in Nevada City, Montana, looked in 1868.

Nat rode up slowly and roped the steer. He pulled it up the hill and outside of town. He rejoined the cowboys. Nat's dad tipped his hat at him. A couple of the other cowboys clapped. Even the trail boss seemed to notice. Nat was thrilled. Finding and roping the steer had been hard work. But he had earned the respect of the other **drovers**. He could almost see his future as a cowboy.

IN THE SADDLE

In the Wild West, almost everyone rode horses. Kids as young as two or three were placed on gentle horses. They were tied in the saddle to learn how to sit. By the time children were five or six, they might have their own ponies. But the ponies were not just for fun. Kids were expected to use them to help with chores.

A 12-year-old girl herds cattle in the early 1900s.

23

Hours later, Billy lay on a straw mattress in the house. He was moaning, and his health was getting worse.

"We should get the doctor," Kate said.

Kate's mother shook her head. "Doc Fuller went to deliver a baby on Tumbleweed Ranch this morning. That's over five miles away."

"That means he won't be back anytime soon," Kate replied with a frown.

THE PONY EXPRESS

Before trains came to the Wild West, long-distance communication was difficult. Telephones had not been invented yet. Sending a message by wagon was slow. A rider was the best way to get in touch with someone. A system called the Pony Express operated from April 1860 through October 1861. It used riders to send mail from town to town. Pony Express riders carried mail from California to Missouri in 10 days, switching riders along the route.

A Pony Express advertisement boasts that letters can be delivered from New York to San Francisco in 10 days.

PONY EXPRESS!

CHANGE OF TIME!   REDUCED RATES!

10 Days to San Francisco!

LETTERS

WILL BE RECEIVED AT THE

OFFICE, 84 BROADWAY,

NEW YORK,

Up to 4 P. M. every TUESDAY,

AND

Up to 2½ P. M. every SATURDAY,

Which will be forwarded to connect with the PONY EXPRESS leaving ST. JOSEPH, Missouri,

Every WEDNESDAY and SATURDAY at 11 P. M.

TELEGRAMS

Sent to Fort Kearney on the mornings of MONDAY and FRIDAY, will connect with PONY leaving St. Joseph, WEDNESDAYS and SATURDAYS.

EXPRESS CHARGES.

LETTERS weighing half ounce or under.............$1 00
For every additional half ounce or fraction of an ounce 1 00
In all cases to be enclosed in 10 cent Government Stamped Envelopes,
And all Express CHARGES Pre-paid.

☞ PONY EXPRESS ENVELOPES For Sale at our Office.

WELLS, FARGO & CO., Ag'ts.

New York, July 1, 1861.

ALSOP & JURGENS, STATIONERS AND PRINTERS, 99 FULTON STREET, NEW YORK.

At sunset, the steers were being loaded onto a train. Nat rode over to Kate.

"Thanks for your help," he said. "How is your brother?"

"He's not well," Kate said. "And Doc Fuller is miles away."

"I can deliver a message," Nat said.

Kate told him where to find the ranch. "I'm glad I can rely on help from friends," she said.

"It's the only way to survive out West," Nat replied.

"Thank you!" Kate called out as Nat rode off, fast as lightning.

CULTURE CLASH

As more settlers moved west, the open plains became dotted with farms and ranches. Wagon trains and cattle drives wove through Native Americans' homelands and hunting grounds. Native Americans relied on buffalo for food and clothing. But cowboys hunted the buffalo until they were almost **extinct**. This created many conflicts between these cultures. Eventually, Native Americans were pushed off their land almost entirely. The Wild West period ended for good in the early 20th century. By then, most of the land had been settled.

Buffalo were once a common sight throughout the West.

Cattle Trail Map

Between 1867 and the mid 1880s about 10 million cattle were herded across the United States in cattle drives. When they reached their destination, the cattle were sold. These are the main routes cowboys and cattle followed.

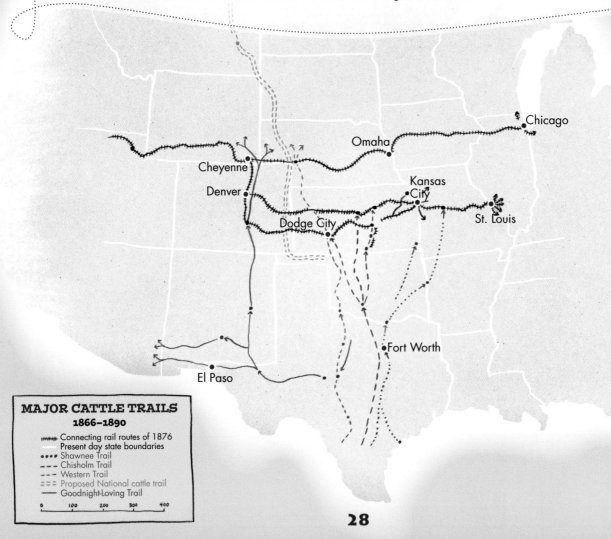

Chicago

Omaha

Cheyenne

Denver

Kansas City

Dodge City

St. Louis

Fort Worth

El Paso

MAJOR CATTLE TRAILS
1866–1890

- ╫╫╫╫ Connecting rail routes of 1876
- ──── Present day state boundaries
- •••• Shawnee Trail
- ---- Chisholm Trail
- – – – Western Trail
- ≡≡≡ Proposed National cattle trail
- ──── Goodnight-Loving Trail

0   100   200   300   400

Timeline

1803 The Louisiana Purchase adds 828,000 square miles (2.1 million square kilometers) of land to the United States in the West.

1830 The Indian Removal Act becomes law. This forces Native Americans out of Oklahoma.

1841 The first wagon trains leave Missouri for the West.

1848 Gold is discovered in California, bringing many more Americans to the West.

1862 The Homestead Act promises Americans free land. As a result, 1.6 million people settle west of the Mississippi River.

1865 The Civil War ends. Many African Americans move to all-black towns in the West.

1869 The first transcontinental railroad is completed. It is built mostly by Chinese immigrants. Most people stop traveling by wagon trains.

1870 Barbed wire fencing becomes popular, and the open plains begin to close to cattle drives.

Words to Know

abolished (uh-BAH-lisht) officially ended

drovers (DROH-vurs) people who move large herds of livestock from place to place

expansion (ik-SPAN-shun) spreading out and enlarging

extinct (ik-STINGKT) no longer found alive

migrated (MYE-gray-tid) moved from one place to another

miracle (MIR-uh-kuhl) an amazing thing that has no obvious explanation

patent medicines (PAT-uhnt MED-uh-sins) products that were sold as medicines, but often did not work as advertised

racism (RAY-siz-uhm) the practice of treating people unfairly or thinking of people differently based on their race

rustlers (RUHS-lurz) people who steal horses, cattle, or sheep

settlers (SET-uh-lurz) people who move to make a home in a new place

Index

ABOUT THE AUTHOR

Tracey Baptiste is the author of the critically acclaimed *Jumbies* series—creepy middle grade fairy tales set in the Caribbean—as well as 12 other fiction and nonfiction books for kids. She is a former classroom teacher, and still loves visiting schools.

ABOUT THE ILLUSTRATOR

Jason Raish is an illustrator living in Brooklyn, New York. He has also lived in Seoul, Beijing, Tokyo, Barcelona, London, and Paris, because new experiences make him a better artist.

Visit this Scholastic website for more information about the Wild West:

www.factsfornow.scholastic.com

Enter the keywords **Wild West**